Heart Songs

by

Mica Rossi

Interior illustrations by Sara Shoemaker

Camelot Publishing Company
PO Box 756
Waukee, IA 50263 U.S.A.
www.camelotpublishingco.com

ISBN 978-1-944442-04-0

Henry, this one is for you

$\mathcal{T}$able of $\mathcal{C}$ontents

Wishing

The rain's patter against the windows is a welcome sound, comforting in its sameness. The way it has sounded all the years of my life. I lay here huddled beneath the blankets in too large a cocoon, wishing you filled the space with me. That this was our own bed in our own house and I had only to say your name and you would answer.

On Becoming Insubstantial

I remember sun on my face and the smell of cut grass and laughter amid a swirl of fireflies in the humid summer darkness. Sometimes the taste of vanilla bean ice cream skims over my lips and tongue again, or dark roast coffee, the kind I used to like. The cool swish of a silk dress against my calves. I remember that.

But I no longer remember myself.

That's what I discovered one morning while I listened to the drumming of the shower through the thin closet walls. A thousand nights I'd asked you to shut the closet door before your shower so you wouldn't waken me. A thousand mornings I awoke to the sound anyway. It wasn't that you were unkind. It was just that you didn't give a damn and so forgot to remember.

It surprised me that I no longer knew who I was. The shock kept me pinned to the mattress the way your body used to. Not that I had forgotten the long-ago me, or even the 'me' of twenty years past. I'd merged with the Mom, and the Mrs., and the Honey, while remaining the Margaret Mary my mother still insisted on.

But the real me, the one that used to live in all the layers of my mind, *that* me had been pressed flat beneath the weight of your body and the reality of our life until there was no me left.

My death happened without fanfare.

I wonder if you noticed at first that I had gone. If you ever questioned what had become of the woman you professed to love. The quirky one, the one who used to squirt you through the kitchen window with the sink hose or spend four hours working on a couplet to place on your pillow before bed. The one who pointed out cloud dinosaurs and held your hand in public. The one who lived.

I guess you didn't notice after all. You would have mentioned it, wouldn't you?

In the dimness of that early October morning, when you opened the bathroom door and then closed the bedroom door behind you, did you miss the still shape no longer in your bed? Or did you follow your morning routine oblivious to the fact that your life had changed before sunrise? You must have seen my car wasn't there. Even you couldn't be that blind.

During the first minutes following my hasty flight, I didn't have time to be scared, only sad that most of my life was gone and I didn't remember living it. Scared came later, after I crept back to the safety of my nest after that failed attempt at leaving it for good. After I realized I had nowhere else to go. After I found myself cleaning up behind you with no more thought in mind than what to take out of the freezer for dinner.

Unsynced

Time disjoined
Ebb and flow inseparable
Rhythm syncopated to anarchy

I walk through lambswool into cotton candy
Balance gone, groping blind
Fingertips to the wall

The banshee warns
Her screech lost in the wind that shoves me
toward the precipice

The rug pulled
Unaware
I whirl into the abyss
Where you wait

Phantom Lover

Between the hours of wake and sleep, you come
to me
Your touch a gentle pressure over my skin and
through the recesses of my mind
Words slide beneath my ribcage to lodge in the
dark places that only you can see
I feel your hands like mist that clings, and long
for more
A kiss, a sigh
I breathe a name that no one hears
and wander into dreams toward my reality

Expelled

"Whatever you do," Mel said, "don't touch that door." It was a plain-looking door, six paneled, made of timeworn mahogany. Nothing special. A door at the end of the second floor hall, just like all the other doors in the house. I never would have given it a second thought if she hadn't pointed it out to me.

"Why? What's behind it?"

"What's behind there would eat you alive."

Her face was grim, the way you would expect a prison warden's face to be, or the doctor's when he came to tell your family you had only three days to live. I'd never seen that expression on anyone so young before, and I wondered what had happened to make her that way. I nearly asked her. I wish now that I had.

She grabbed her purse from the hall table and got a good grip on her suitcase, hefting it up in a way that suggested solid weight, although her shoulders didn't tilt with the effort. I admired that, the fact that she could carry that bag without leaning. I don't know why except that I'd always been something of a weakling when it came to upper body strength.

She stalked out the front door without looking back. I watched her sling the suitcase into the back seat and slam the door shut. The car roared off in a shower of gravel. I thought I saw her wave, but I couldn't be sure. The glimpse I had of the side of her face suggested an eagerness to be away from here, a certain lightening of the grimness.

The keys Mel had left me jingled in my hand, reminding me of the phone ringing several days before when she'd called me.

"Chrissy, I know it's short notice," she'd said, "but do you think you could housesit for me tomorrow through next week? And take care of the dogs? I'd be willing to pay you."

Of course, starving student that I was, I agreed right away. I loved Mel's dogs, and I loved her house, an old Victorian affair with gables and gingerbread and turreted rooms. She'd had the good sense to hire an expert in Victorian restoration. The result was elegant without being stuffy and authentic without being gloomy. I always felt I'd stepped back in time when I entered the foyer and was mildly surprised that a parlor maid didn't ask if I wanted tea in the drawing room. If you please, Mum.

Connor, a Golden-Australian mix, and Salsa, a year old chocolate Lab, danced around my legs as I wandered through the main hallway and up the stairs. Mel had put me in the Burgundy Room, a fairy concoction of deep velvet draperies and lace-edged sheets, comfortable stuffed chairs and a fireplace large enough to hold a roasted ox. The dressing table was stocked with perfumes and powders and a silver brush and comb set Mel had found at one of the interminable auctions she was forever attending. I sat and brushed out my dark hair, feeling like the heroine in a movie.

When I placed the brush back on the table, I knocked the keys to the floor. The ring held keys to every room in the house, including the door Mel said not to touch.

Salsa's whine distracted me from forbidden temptations. I dropped the keyring into my jacket pocket and let the dogs out into the back for a run. Mel lived along the shore of a lake, and the retrievers took off like a shot for the water. We played fetch the stick for about an hour. By the time the sun starting sinking, I was as wet as the dogs. The exercise felt great, and I'd had fun, but I couldn't get the thought of that door out of my mind. Why had Mel said not to open it?

I thought about the door and the room behind it while I took a shower, and later when I made a simple salad and heated a bowl of soup for dinner, and later yet when I started a fire in the front parlor. The ring of keys made a bulge in the pocket of my terry-cloth robe. A cup of tea didn't help me to ignore them, and neither did the book I pulled from the library shelf. Close to midnight, I gave up trying to read and laid the book on the table next to my chair.

The fire had died down to glowing embers. Salsa lay in front of the hearth. Connor had taken up residence over my feet and seemed reluctant to move when I stood. They both stretched and walked, one on each side of me, up the stairway. When I turned left toward that room at the end of the hall, I realized that neither of them had stayed with me but waited at the door to my own room.

"Come on, you guys. What's the problem?"

Connor growled low in his throat but didn't move. Salsa stayed quiet until I took the keys from my pocket, and then she added her growl to Connor's. A house didn't have to fall on me. The dogs didn't want me going into that room. Common sense told me they were probably right. I shouldn't be doing this. Mel had warned me. The dogs warned me now, but curiosity won out.

The key slid easily into the lock and turned with little effort. Light spilled around the edges of the door, golden light that made me catch my breath with its beauty. I pulled the door wide.

Without conscious volition, I found myself walking forward into the garden. The earth felt soft beneath my feet, and the warmth of the light caressed my skin. It was several moments before I realized that my clothing had melted away, but I didn't care. I felt right naked in this place. There was nothing sensual about my nudity, but rather a joyful innocence that had always been and always would be.

Smells overwhelmed me, the flowers and the leaves, the grass underfoot. I had never smelled such riches before. They lay on my tongue heavy enough to taste. Colors sparkled, their brilliance indescribable. Wind played through the luxuriant growth around me, touching my body with delicate fingers before drifting away.

The tree grew in the middle of the path before me. I knew that tree. I'd heard about it every Sunday from the time I was a little girl in Bible School. It was a beautiful tree, tall and stately. The fruit hanging from its branches was plump and ripe, bursting with color and with a sweetness I could smell. The figure draped over the trunk was neither serpent nor ugly. He was gorgeous.

The force of his gaze pulled my eyes upward toward his and kept them locked there. I felt heat within my loins, heat that spread slowly from between my legs to my belly and higher. My breasts tingled, as if his hands had slid over my flesh, arousing the nipples to hardness, exquisite pain that only he could assuage. I swear his tongue darted over my lips although several feet separated us. His eyes promised passion and fulfillment, an end to the aching need that burned within. When he held the fruit out to me, I bit into it without hesitation.

The light died. Vegetation withered and the wind that moments before had delighted me now scoured me with sand and pebbles. Banshees screamed around my head, driving me toward the cracked and broken door through which I'd entered the garden. I stumbled through and fell to the wooden floor. The door slammed shut behind me and the dogs were there, licking the tears streaming across my cheeks.

I don't know how many days I spent in that position. When I woke, I found the dogs close against me and weak sunlight dotting the upper hall through open doors. Hunger cramped my stomach but didn't match the emptiness gnawing at my soul.

In the cool air of the house, I shivered and stretched, making my way to my room on legs that barely held me up. I almost didn't recognize the girl who looked back at me when I passed the dressing table, the one whose face wore a grimness I'd seen recently on another face.

Mel had been thrown out of Eden too.

Until We Get It Right

how many lifetimes we've done this before
it all turns out the same
no matter that I get burned and swear no more

helpless to resist, I let the lodestone draw me in
you die, I die, fate sends us back
and we begin again

Love a While Longer

Some days you think about moving on
Wishing you were already gone
But he says the words that make it real
And you can't deny what you feel
So you learn to deal

Everyone else gets a piece of his time
And you get pushed to the back of the line
Though he's promised you a wedding band
He makes you feel like a one-night-stand
But you love the man

He doesn't need you and your heart aches
You keep on hoping while your life breaks
'Cause when he remembers to want you
He's that much closer to a break through
So you make do

You wander, lost, from room to room
The house is colder than an empty tomb
He's always gone, you don't know where

Just forgets you're even there
'Cause he doesn't care

Step back and take a look from outside
Don't let him take you on such a wild ride
You knew you'd have to make this choice
eventually
When will you choose reality?

You find you're nearly done and then
He says three little words again
And you love a while longer

Handfast

In the stillness of night
By the dark of the moon
If I chance upon your dreams
Will you bid me enter?

In the soft of the morning
By the pale of the sky
If I hold out my hand
Will you walk my way?

In the sequence of our years
By the promise spoken now
If I give you my heart
Will you stay forever?

Reformation

"Hi, my name is Casey, and my daughter is an alcoholic." I said it quietly. I don't know how many of those around me heard what I said, and I'm sure those in the back of the room couldn't hear me at all, but the sea of faces looked at me with sympathy.

"Hi, Casey."

The chorus of voices was comforting. I had sat here week after week, trying to find out what drew people to these meetings, what possessed them to stand in front of this group of more than fifty people and spew their emotions. Some of them were nervous. Some cried. Some were shaking so badly, they could barely stand. One woman clutched the arm of the man next to her for support while she talked.

There were sounds of agreement when people spoke, and pats of encouragement. The faces in the crowd were those of strangers, but they promised an ear to listen, a heart to hear, a sorrow shared. They had all been there.

I listened to their stories, trying to find fodder for the article I had come to write, about what my husband called the "groupsy-woopsy" nature of Al-Anon. I had come to scoff at these individuals, some old, some young, all heartbroken and searching for help. For acceptance. Maybe for hope. I had come to scoff and expose. Instead, I took a deep breath and got ready to tell my story.

Creation

within these pages
you are mine

Friend

Champion

Hero

your loyalty is absolute
a steadfast wall at my back
the stone from which I draw my strength
chapters fly by
you become

Life

Lover

All

$\mathcal{L}$ifelines

Call me Ishmael. I probably won't answer. I hate the name, but my mom had a love affair with a book instead of my dad, so I got stuck with Ishmael instead of Robert, Jr. What can I say?

She was always reading me bits and pieces out of books. Lines as long as my arm with the words climbing one on top of the other until they were piled so deep that you got stuck in the image whether you wanted to or not. I always pretended boredom, but I lived for those quiet times when the words that fell between us evoked other places where we could hide from the here and now.

"Ish," she would say (she always called me that), "we're off to London tonight," and her voice would change, become crisp and precise, the way I remembered from old radio broadcasts during Before, but without the shrill panic of those days. We got caught up in the Dodger's antics, and when she stopped, in my head I echoed Oliver's plaintive "please, sir, I want some more." I never let her know how much I liked it.

She was real sick during After. Sometimes she could barely hold the book, even resting it on her knees while she sat. She refused to get into the bed.

"I get in there, I'll never get out," she'd say.

I watched her get thinner and thinner, and drag herself from the chair to the window, from the window to the crapper. I'd hear her gagging in there and know that she was losing what little I'd been able to steal on the streets for us to eat. But every night if I was there, she'd haul up whatever book we'd been reading and start in again.

"Promise me you'll hold onto the books," she'd say, and I'd promise without looking at her, knowing that if she died, I'd sell those things in a heartbeat to get some decent food to eat. We'd argued about it in the beginning, about

how the books had gone up in smoke and flames
and when there weren't any more, people
realized what they'd never have again. One
book would have brought her enough food and
pills to make her well. But she wouldn't.

"They're my lifeline," she'd say.

"You don't let me sell one of these, you won't
have no life left," I'd say.

"*Any* life," she'd say, and that would be the end
of it.

I thought about sneaking one out, some night
when she was asleep in that chair and wrapped
in every scurvy-looking blanket we had. But
somehow, knowing that she'd know what I'd
done, I just couldn't do it. Not even to save her.

So this is what I'm left with. *Moby Dick* and
Oliver Twist and ten or twelve others. A king's
ransom in paper.

I carried her down to the knacker when he rolled
through town, his cart wheels scraping sparks
off the broken pavement.

"Bring out your dead," he'd call.

Just like in some book she'd told me about before the Before. Something about plagues and people falling like stones and just laying where they fell. Like she fell last night, the book weighing her down so much that she couldn't stay upright. I carried her to the chair, her and the book both, and she probably weighed the least. She'd hurt her wrist real bad. I could see it bent a way I didn't think it should be, but she laid that book in her lap and had me hold down one edge while she turned to the first page.

"Scarlett O'Hara was not beautiful, but men seldom realized it when caught by her charm as the Tarleton twins were." Her voice became soft and slow, and in it I heard magnolias and the whisper of petticoats, and the sweet, Southern cadence of days gone by.

"Do you wish you lived then," I said when she stopped. She never answered. Her hand rested on the page, her head tipped forward as if she'd fallen asleep. But she wasn't asleep.

And so she is gone and I am left with the choice of living well or not. I had the book in my hand, fat and heavy with the magic and horror of that period in the Way Before, and I couldn't do it. Halfway out the door, I knew I couldn't.

I pulled the chair over next to the light fading through the window, and the tears ran while I listened with Scarlett as she heard her first rebel yell.

Where We Used to Be

I liked it there
The place we used to be
Me
You
No complacency
The path before us undefined
Possibilities endless
Together in a way we aren't anymore
Now we walk between narrow hedges
Looking neither left nor right
Nor at each other
Only straight ahead to the ending

$\mathcal{F}$etters

In August, the year her middle child, Brian, had the chicken pox, when the temperature outside fueled the heat of her emotions, she wrote:

Dear Sam,

I hate you and I hate what you've turned me into. I'm sorry I ever met you. I'm equally sorry I let you decide for me that having three kids, quitting my job and giving up my dream of going to school were good things. I wish you were dead, but that would leave me penniless and unable to care for your children. As soon as I can afford it, I'm walking out the door to recapture my life.

She folded the note in thirds and sealed it in an envelope, laying it on the smoothly covered pillows of her bed where Sam would be sure to see it as soon as he came home from work. Three hours later, Brian got up from his nap so quietly that Sarah never heard him. She found the three-year-old sitting on the bed, chewing on the envelope.

Sarah cried that day, pulling the soggy letter from her son's mouth and rocking the baby in her arms while Brian patted his mama's wet cheeks. That same week, and once or twice in the following month, Sarah tried to compose another letter, but the burning desire to change her life had cooled. She let the decision to leave slide beneath the mountains of laundry and the cereal crusted onto the breakfast bowls.

In May the year her oldest child graduated, with the realization that she'd used up half her life, she wrote.

Dear Sam,

I hate you and I hate what I've let myself turn into. I'm sorry I ever met you. I'm equally sorry that I didn't decide to keep my job and my dream of going to school. I'd wish I were dead, but that wouldn't solve anything. I'm moving out before any more time passes and I can't ever recapture my life.

She folded the note and sealed it in an envelope, placing it on the dining room table where Sam would be sure to see it when they returned from the graduation ceremony. Daniel brought it to her that night, his face white and drawn, his hand shaking. It had gotten mixed up with his graduation cards and he'd opened it, reading it through before recognizing what he held.

Sarah cried that day also, rocking Daniel in her arms while her tears mingled with his, trying to explain between gasping breaths that it was her jealousy talking, that she envied him his whole life to do what he dreamed of, that she would never consider separating from his father. She soothed the boy's hurt, burying her decision to leave under the blanket of lies she told for her son's sake.

In December of the year before her youngest daughter's wedding, with the boxes of decorations and ornaments opened around her, Jamie's wedding gown spread across the sofa, she wrote:

Dear Sam,

I don't hate you or me anymore, but I do hate what I've let myself become. I'm not sorry I ever met you. You've been a solid rock in the world of my indecision. I'm only sorry that I couldn't make up my mind about what I wanted, what I needed, what I dreamed of. Now I know all those things and it's too late to recapture my life.

When Sarah cried that day, she did it softly, the tears dripping off her chin to wet her green silk blouse. Then she wiped her face, burned the letter in the fireplace and gathered up a handful of ornaments to decorate the tree, sinking her desires into the ocean of fear she'd built over her lifetime.

3.24 a.m.

Sleepless
Though you're still here
Soon I will not be
When dawn rises
So too will I and there will be
Miles and hours between us again
Your arm tightens around me
I curl into your warmth
And decide to let the dawn take care of itself

Storms

Gran always said that the best and the worst things got carried in on the wings of a storm. At seventeen, she met my grandfather the night her car ran into a ditch during a thunderstorm. And once a twister deposited a patio table, unscathed, in her back yard. Those were good things.

The night I was born was a good and a bad thing at the same time. A freak electrical storm happened as my mom and dad made a mad dash for the hospital. Usually these storms are harmless light shows, but this night there must have been some real lightning hiding up in the clouds because a bolt of it hit a tree just as my father drove under it. Mom had me in the back seat while Dad lay crushed in the front. They named me Stephanie after my father, and every time Gran called me 'Stevie,' I could see her eyes brighten.

At twenty-four, I'm sure I haven't lived long enough to see the very best or worst I'll ever see during my life, but I've seen some weird stuff during storms. Gran said it's part of my gift, the ability to see things most people don't. I'm not certain 'gift' is the word I'd use, though. Sometimes 'curse' is closer to the truth.

Like the spring before last. For weeks I'd been feeling on edge, nothing that I could put my finger to, just a vague sense that things felt off. The feeling intensified toward the end of April. Until the night of the 'Big Storm.' That's how people around here refer to it.

The heat built that morning from a mild sixty degrees to a stifling eighty-nine by noon. Thunderclouds rolled in, piling in drifts tall enough to reach heaven. The humidity climbed higher than the temperature until the storm let loose with a bang that shook the rafters of the old house Gran and Mom and I lived in.

Since it was the weekend, I didn't have to work. I'd curled up in the window seat overlooking the old cemetery on the west edge of our property. This had been my favorite spot from earliest childhood, a place I could indulge my bookish nature with the fantasies and fairytales that I loved. Strangely, I also liked history and had read everything the library had to offer in the way of local historical data. The cemetery became my playground, with its fascinating headstones from the early 1800's. It wasn't much used anymore, but I had gotten to know its residents in the pages of the books I read about the town's ancestors.

For the most part, they were a hardworking bunch of citizens, trying to eke out a living from the rich Midwestern soil. Occasionally, a bad guy would drift in, cause some trouble and either drift back out or end up in Rosewood Cemetery, off to one side away from the locals. The accounts of the residents might have seemed boring to some, but they captured my pioneer spirit, plunging my imagination into a world of wood-burning stoves and buggy wheels.

My head snapped up from the pages of a book as the storm announced itself, my eyes drawn through the deluge to the strange figure cavorting through the graveyard. He danced from one tombstone to another, sinking to the ground atop a grave before leaping up and on to the next stone. I closed the book and hurried down the stairs, meaning to yell at whoever it was, but by the time I reached the side of our wrap-around porch, he'd disappeared.

Other figures had taken his place though, climbing from beneath the earth as if getting out of bed in the morning. There was Lily Conley, the town whore, dressed in bright green satin. She shook out the folds of her dress, brushing at a bit of earth sticking near the scandalously short hem before looking around with an eager smile. Timothy Winters came up next, his longish hair falling over one eye. His biceps bulged in the simple denim shirt he wore. He held out a hand to Lily, helping her over her own simple grave marker and sweeping her into his arms for a lengthy kiss.

Timothy's father climbed out, a murderous look on his face when he saw Tim and Lily locked in an embrace. He pulled a shovel from the ground beneath him and strode across the cemetery to push Lily from his son's side. The shovel swung up over his head and he brought it down on the back of Lily's neck. I saw Tim's mouth open in a howl, although I couldn't hear anything but the crashing of thunder and the rain as it roared through the gutters and downspouts. His huge hands closed around his father's neck and squeezed. Mr. Winters' fingers clawed at his son's, but Timothy just shook his father like a dog shakes a knotted sock. When Tim dropped his father on the ground, Mr. Winters lay where he fell, his head twisted at a grotesque angle.

Sheriff Newland popped up, both fists closed around a rifle. He shot Timothy in the stomach. I could see the fire flash from the rifle's mouth but again, heard nothing. Someone else shot the Sheriff. The bullet came from one of the graves where the drifters went along the outside edge of the graveyard. Others came up, so fast that I couldn't see from which grave. Some of them stripped off their clothes, men and women coupling on the muddy ground. Husbands killed their wives, wives killed their children.

The town's printed history floated through my head. A lie. It had all been a lie. Somehow, I knew what I saw was the truth. Beneath the ground lay the most depraved of souls, and the storm had loosed them upon the earth.

I covered my face, squeezing my eyes shut against the macabre scene before me. The storm passed through quickly, and when I dropped my hands, the figures seeped back into the ground.

I think Timothy Winters winked at me.

Anything I Say

No deep thoughts, just surface talk
And you don't call me baby anymore
The thrill is gone, the days roll on
I feel you getting closer to the door

I want to do a replay of our first day
That breathless, helpless falling into us
Letting you in, getting tangled in skin
Hungry for love and learning to trust

I know you're living a lie, baby so am I
We go through the motions that don't mean a
thing
Kisses in the air, but we don't really care
Ritual alone, love dangled from a string

Can't we go back to then, begin again
Make this life happen a whole different way
Together, not apart, make a new start
A change from same thing, new day

Don't want to regret it, can't seem to forget it
Maybe we can find the road back to each other
As it stands, I'm lost, can't count the cost
I can't make it work without you, lover

But we all dance to the music of time
Trying to find the words to save what's mine
Keep what's left of us but don't know how
Because anything I say right now
Will sound like good-bye

Waiting in the Wings

I tell myself I won't do this anymore
Won't wait until you have time to notice me
to spend an hour with me
to love me
Until you have time to even think about me
I know I'm worth more than this
And yet…
I allow my pain to leach unremarked into my
pillow
My heart stands quietly in the wings
and when my cue comes
mask in place
lines learned
I play my part to your world

Awakening

The lust for red meat finally roused her. She sniffed the night air, trying to identify scents alien yet oddly familiar. Vegetation with an undercurrent of rot. Rabbit. And there, blood.

A strange wailing far in the distance and the beat of wings overhead thrummed against hypersensitive eardrums. With a nearly inaudible whine, she crept from her hiding place beneath the leaves, stepping carefully on sore paws. Her flanks heaved, bones showing stark through her rough coat.

She didn't know this place or recall how she'd gotten here. Weird images flashed through her head, of men and machines, stone and metal towers. Shouted sounds – words? – and the sharp smell of fear flashed, a memory of sorts. There were stronger memories, primal, of her teeth tearing flesh and a taste, the sweet, hot nectar of blood on her tongue.

Again she whined, louder, lost in a jumble of incomplete thoughts, unanswered questions half-formed. Reason pulled her toward the city. Instinct drove her away and so she stayed rooted, until hunger banished both reason and instinct.

The undergrowth rustled not far off. Ears forward, stiff-legged, she turned toward the source, her overwhelming need for food urging her to abandon caution. Uncertain of her abilities, she peered through the brush, her eyes shining orange in the moonlight. Saliva ran from her muzzle. When a porcupine waddled into view, she fought the impulse to pounce, forcing herself to seek a less dangerous meal.

Putting her nose to the ground, she followed a rabbit's trail, flushing it into the open, but she couldn't sustain the pace needed to catch it. Her belly rumbled and her legs folded under her. She howled, a long, mournful sound that split the sky with despair. The echoes answered her, and she raised her head and listened. Not an echo, a voice calling back to her. She didn't know the voice of this beast, but she recognized its scent on the wind. Safety lay in that scent.

A picture formed in her mind, of red-gold eyes surrounded by pale gray fur. Comfort came with the image and a word. Mate. Willing her legs to obey, she staggered deeper into the wood, stalking the scent that drew her. She stumbled and rose, pushing her body until she could rise no longer.

The sun against her face woke her much later. Dreams and half-formed recollections teased her, of flesh yielding to her bite, of eyes watching her as she ate her fill. A rough tongue that eased the pain of her ragged paws and licked the blood from her muzzle.

Leaves crackled as she turned, exposing heated flank skin to cool morning air. She lay naked, nestled against a warm chest hard against her softness. Legs tangled with hers. She had a fleeting image of thick fur on a lean body as she twined one arm around the man's neck. He stirred, looking deep into her eyes before his arms cradled her.

"Good morning, love," he said. "Welcome to my world."

Voted Most Popular

elegance, beauty, poetry walking
tall and sleek
golden cream sculpted within designer jeans
bursting resplendent from her Beemer cocoon at
morning bell
feathered fall of cornsilk hair
a waft of fragrance
saccharin voice dripping honeyed barbs

we knew our doom
moths to the flame
willing victims for a glimpse of grace
a glimmer of hope
naked in our ugliness
supplicants
we held our breaths when she passed
beseeching a look
benediction

no glance of pity for those who scourged their
souls on her edges
no glance at all

Being

"You don't have a choice, Jen."

Those are the first words I hear when I awake from insensibility. I'm not sure where I am, but it's warm here, and comfortable. Sound is a new thing in this dark place, a strange sensation that tickles the inside of my head. It's different from what I've known before, and I'm not sure I like it. It disturbs me somehow, because along with the muffled sound comes a rise in the temperature and a prickling along my back and neck. The dull thudding that I felt long before this increases in tempo and reverberates through my skull.

"Not if you want me to stay around."

Nope, I don't like sound at all. Its absence was much nicer. The harsh voice chills me in this warm home, and I want it to go away.

"Michael."

A different voice now. Softer. Sweeter. I like this one. It's soothing.

"I mean it. I won't get roped into this. I can't give up my scholarship next year. If you do this, you do it on your own."

A big bang, and a tremor goes through this place where I am. The nasty voice is quiet, but I hear another sound, one that makes my heart ache. Love wells up in me. The aching sound comes from the soothing voice. It makes me ache as well. The thudding echoes with a deep, frantic pulse, and my own heart races along in time. I feel changes within this space, currents once calm that rush and roar around and through me, tumbling me end over end with grief.

Finally, the aching sounds still. The thudding slows.

"What am I going to do?"

The whisper floats along the liquid cradling me, and again love fills me, spilling outward. I long to touch that voice, to hear it clear and unshrouded, and I reach out toward it, but encounter only emptiness. I have not yet defined the limitations of my place here.

Love drives me to try again, pushes me to connect with the object of my love. I feel insignificant, the space around me cavernous, but I stretch and move until my hand brushes something solid, once and then again.

All movement stops. My place becomes quiescent, its turbulence becalmed. The surface I rest against warms from the outside.

"He's right. I have no choice." The voice enfolds me with tenderness. "I love you already."

Wrapped in that soft blanket of emotion, I go back to sleep.

Changling

'Neath waning moon and velvet sky
she passes
Searching for the one she never knew
But ever seeks
Within the ring of dancing lads and lasses
She touches each face with hope
But seldom speaks
When her mortal sojourn has
reached it ending
Yet young she is and lovely
As daybreak turns to night
Will he not come,
reveal himself, attending
This changling fairy child
Before she leaves the light?

*E*yes of the Beholder

She smelled of peppermint, her cheeks sunken, scanty white hair spread over the pillow in a nimbus. I was sure she didn't know me anymore. She'd never say my name again, or wink at me out of deep blue eyes. I'd never again shiver as her lips parted in that slow smile reserved for me alone. Although she'd been the same for the last several months, today, for the first time, I knew the Reaper had ahold of her.

Where had she gone, my best friend, the bright, sweet schoolgirl, the matron with her gentle smile, the lovely older woman who'd shared the last twenty years with me? In my mind's eye, the hand that smoothed her hair wasn't gnarled and spotted, and the hair it stroked was black and lustrous. Silent tears slipped over my cheeks, and my heavy heart reached back for happier days, earlier days.

Her hand crept over the blanket, clutching, twisting, coming to rest on my knee. Bent fingers stiff with disease, but such a delicate touch. The slightest pressure of her fingertips against my neck had thrilled me; the hint of perfume on her wrist heightened my senses. Her mouth delivered riches.

I had known her all my life. Celia had a part in my earliest memories. We shared our ice cream with each other first, and later, our kisses. She began where I ended, the continuation of my soul.

As I wiped the tears from my face, her hand slid from my knee, dangling over the edge of the bed. Gently, I placed it next to her side and held it, my thumb stroking the smooth skin near her thumb. She gave a great sigh, like a contented child nuzzling against its mother at bedtime, and her fingers squeezed my hand with barely enough strength to be felt. I was mesmerized by the slight rise and fall of her breast beneath the sheets. Her hand squeezed again, a little harder, and I raised my eyes to her face.

The ravages of time could not erase the dainty bone structure beneath her wrinkled skin, still porcelain white. The tip of her tongue worked to moisten cracked lips, and I hastened to apply a glycerin swab, releasing another wave of peppermint scent into the air. Her breathing quickened and then slowed again, becoming labored. The swab dropped to the bed, where it made a small, wet circle against the green blanket. I reached my hand to her cheek, cradling its softness against my palm as she struggled for air.

Her eyes opened and she looked at me, really saw me for the first time in a long time. She looked at me with love, and pride, and remembrance. She looked at me with concern, and respect, and peace. She looked at me with longing, and regret, and farewell.

And then she winked.

Christmas Through My Eyes

Sense of wonder
Innocence
The ability to believe
Gone
You wander alone in a cold storm
Searching for safe and warm
For this one time
Let me show you the way it used to be
When you were a child and all was possible
I have love enough to take you
All the way to Christmas through my eyes

Don't Forget Me

I am your brother, your mother, your sister, your aunt, uncle and cousin, your father.

I am a passenger on the planes, the staff at the Pentagon, the employee and visitor in the twin towers.

I am the firefighter, police officer and medical personnel who went into danger to help those in need.

Don't forget me.

I am the doctor, the nurse, the EMT and medic, the soldier, the sailor, one of the caring thousands who gave my time, my love and my help because that's all I had to give. I am one of those left behind, looking inward at my shattered life and outward at the shattered landscape of terror. I am your neighbor, your friend. Your family. I am the widow and widower, orphan, and homeless. I am your blood. I am an American.

In the days and weeks and months and years to come, when you play with your dog or cuddle your child; when you barbeque in the back yard or watch television, brush your hair, pound the keyboard; when you visit your uncle in Richmond or vacation with your wife in California; when you put flowers on a grave or say a prayer; when you see Old Glory unfurl in the breeze of a perfect summer's day…

Don't forget me.

$\int$weat

Child: I felt it dripping down my back as I walked across the stage. The floorboards beneath my feet seemed miles long, disappearing into the blackness outside the spotlight's glare. I'd never make it to the bench. My knees began to tremble as that maddening trickle made its way between my shoulder blades, gliding over the downy hairs on my back. I wanted to scratch at the tickling, cram my fingers beneath the stiff, pink taffeta dress. I could feel that tiny bead of water slipping lower, toward my waist, disappearing to join its friends in the elastic band of my panties. The piano gleamed as the spotlight struck its polished surface. I collapsed onto the bench, drew a deep breath and began to play.

Teen: I felt it sticking beneath my arms as I waltzed down the stairs. The carpeting softened the tapping of my high heels to muffled thuds. I worried the midnight blue velvet of my dress would display a darker color, make visible my nervousness, as if my fingers clamped around my beaded bag hadn't already betrayed me. Did I dare pull the fabric away from my skin? No, that would totally gross everyone out. How long had we been walking down these stairs? A bead of water broke loose and skimmed over my ribcage. Was it leaving a mark? As we hit the dance floor, music started and I drew a deep breath, floating off in the arms of my date.

Bride: I felt it dampening my nylons as I took measured steps down the aisle. Dad's arm felt rock hard beneath my hand. I clutched that solid surface with desperate, eager fingers, reluctant to let go, yearning to let go. My legs caressed the white satin of my gown. Would it be stained by the moisture? One bead of water slid down the concave skin behind my knee, over my calf, to lose itself in the hollow of my ankle. My father gave me a kiss and let go. I turned toward my future, drew a deep breath and smiled.

Mother: I felt it slicking the surface of my face and neck, drenching my chest as I careened through the halls. The delivery room doors had shrunk to a pinpoint at the end of a long tunnel.

I'd never make it to the table. My green hospital gown stuck to my belly and breasts. The gurney's wheels squeaked with each revolution, audible accompaniment to my internal chant - pant, don't push, pant, don't push, not yet, not yet. A fresh cachet of water slid from my neck to join the pool at my back. Doors crashed against walls. Bright lights struck my eyes and I drew a deep breath and pushed.

Empty Nester: I felt it saturating my T-shirt as I carried her boxes along the dorm corridor. Her room seemed much too close to the doors. I wanted to linger with each trip to the parking lot, make the day last longer. My baby, my little one. The summer sun drew forth my love with my body's moisture. One little bead crept from my temple to mingle with the water on my cheeks. Just hot, I assured her, wiping away the telltale signs. I drew a deep breath and gave her freedom.

Grandmother: I felt it dripping over my forehead as I chased him over the grass. The soccer ball was just a blur between his feet, the goal too far away for me to catch him before he got there. The drip became a steady torrent that plastered my shortened hair to my skull. I drew a deep breath, and drew another deep breath, and another, and went for some lemonade.

Widow: I felt it wetting my whole body, encasing me in a clammy pall of sorrow as I followed the casket toward his grave. It seeped into my widow's weeds, molding the cotton to my bony frame. I drew a deep breath, stifling the scream that threatened to break free from my soul, and said good-bye.

Dying: I felt nothing anymore as I lay on my bed. No slickening, no slipping, no damping, saturating, dripping, sticking. My body had dried out, no moisture left. No life left. I drifted between this world and the next, mostly alone. Until my great-granddaughter entered my room and held my hand, her palm blessing mine with her sweat. Through bleary eyes, I watched her tender smile, gripping her hand for that last touch of life. I drew a deep...

Everywhere

I find you in the strangest things
In rain and wind
In the storm-laden clouds roiling above my head
In the sound of thunder that rolls a thousand
bass drums deep across the sky
In the waves that crash over my feet and the tide
that pulls me closer to you
In the open road that beckons me on
In the stretch of the cat and the sunlight slanting
across timeworn floors
In the smell of carnations, spicy sharp and sweet
In the child's laugh and the stranger's smile
And every single time I chance across a pair of
eyes as deep and quiet as a forest glen at sunfall.

Out of the Shadows

I crawled out of the shadows my life had cast me into at 3:47 a.m. on March 3, 1954. I remember the exact date and time, because the dog started howling at 3:42, pushing me out of the nightmarish world I'd inhabited every waking or sleeping moment since my eighth birthday. The year my mother died. The year my father sold me to Jacob Peters to pay for a new tractor. The year I became a statistic.

I wasn't asleep when Boomer howled. I didn't sleep much, even though a bunch of time had passed since Jacob Peter's death. This house, the only home I'd known for more years than I could count, held most of the shadows I'd lived in, but I'd stayed, having nowhere else to go. Boomer had shown up on my doorstep one afternoon, a scraggly, starving mutt, shivering in the rain. I'd taken him in and in return, he loved me unconditionally, something I hadn't had since before my mother died. He never barked, didn't make much in the way of noise at all, so when he started howling, I jumped out of the cocoon of sheets and blankets I'd buried myself in. The clock said 3:42. Exactly five minutes later, I found Annie.

The Appalachians weren't much populated back then. Still aren't but neighbors were scarcer at that time. Jacob Peter's cabin was in an isolated valley, hemmed in by a ring of mountains and one swiftly moving creek that crept too near the back door for comfort during the spring. Snow lay thick on the ground, sometimes past my hips. How the child came to be there, I've never discovered. She doesn't remember. I think she doesn't want to yet. I think she still dreams about it, night terrors that fill the house with her screams and soak the sheets with her tears. The shadows that fill her life.

I don't know how old she was then. Maybe six or seven, maybe older. It was hard to tell, she was so skinny, and her leg had been broken and set bad, shortening her frame to accommodate the limp. She had no hair. Someone had shaved it off, all over her body. Later it grew in on her head, a deep, shiny brown that reminded me of ripe chestnuts. But that night she looked like the picture of a gnome my mother had shown me once in a book of fairy stories, all bald and wizened and scrawny.

She was frozen near through, only one shoe on and just a light summer dress, a rough brown blanket wrapped around her, the kind they used in the Army. We'd had some of those once that Daddy had bought at the surplus store. I think it was all that kept her from freezing. For a while, I was afraid she'd lose her toes, but somehow, she kept 'em.

She'd been beaten within an inch of her life. And although she never said, I think she'd been raped repeatedly. I saw myself when I looked in her face, the little girl I'd been, the one who had lived in the shadows of the past until 3:47 a.m. that cold night. I couldn't stay in them after seeing her.

Only someone who'd lived in the shadows could help Annie find her way out.

For My Godmother

I wore your shoes when I was little
marveling at the perfection of their fit
though I was only eight and you were grown
I thought I filled your shoes
but later came to know that I could not
You were my aunt, and my godmother
You were my friend

Time did not change the small, bright person
that you were
Despite the trials and tribulations
you were given to bear
you stood always proud and upright
your eyes and soul as bright as a child's
as warm and comfortable as a pair of old
slippers
that you put on after easing off the three-inch
heels
you always wore

Your absence leaves a void slowly filling with
your memories
There is no comfort in those
Not yet
It is too soon
But some near day
I will see you as I always have
In your shorts and sandals
with your hair pulled back in a ponytail
your face alight with laughter and love
as you push your young daughter's swing higher
It is the picture of you that I have carried around
in my heart
the one that comes to mind when I hear your
name

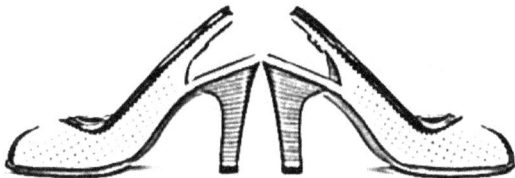

Fly with Me

In the night beyond the gloaming
Before dawning has its time
I can sense your spirit roaming
And your thoughts reach out to mine

Distance is no measure
Of the heat I feel from you
Or the wanting and the needing
Soaring passion, strong and true

Your face is at my window
As your eyes pierce through my dreams
I try to bid you enter
Not as easy as it seems

I lie here in my prison
Strain against these earthly chains
To join you in your dance among the clouds
Yet make no gains

But my heart will do your bidding
When you touch it, wild and free
I will heed your whispered longing
Oh, my lover, fly with me

Heart Song

In the quiet I have found
a life
your love
our souls
my heart
this us

If Only

What if I had met you sooner
Turned that corner all those years ago
Walked down Fifth instead of Main
Put on a slicker and braved the rain

What if we had bumped into each other
Maybe in that coffee shop we both know
Or the little café just down the street
If only circumstances had let us meet

What if you and I had said hello
On the bus or at some crowded corner stop
If your eyes became caught up in mine
Would we still have wasted all this time

What if our paths had crossed before
Entanglements in other lives
Would you have known that you belonged with
me
If only you and I had become we…

Lament

When did we become memory?
Us in past tense
Your image retreats
The footage interrupted, off track
The tilt of your head, the look in your eyes
Becomes
Muted, soft-focused
A time-worn Polaroid square
Blurred still-life
Until I can't remember
Us

Images

I saw white horses running, running, prancing
White
manes
dancing
White
nostrils
flared
Snorting
clouds of
white mist
Leaping and falling
Chasing each other back and forward
Running toward me
All around
Until they crashed with great noise on the beach
And turned to foam over my feet

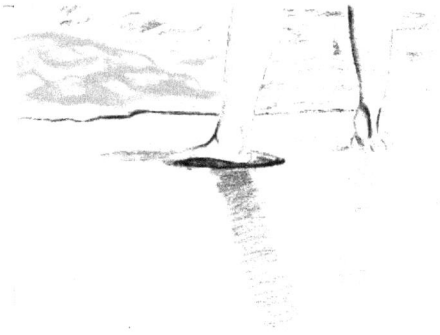

In My Defense

If I had to name just what we have, I couldn't
It's the strangest kind of love I've ever seen
Seldom near, barely touched
Yet I'm loving you so much
That loving you makes perfect sense
In my defense

I'm all caught up in feelings of 'I shouldn't'
But babe, against your love there's no vaccine
Say I'm crazy, you'd be right
But in the quiet of the night
Loving you makes perfect sense
In my defense

Intensity

So bad for each other
Remember
My anger flew without regard
For your pride
Your words bit without regard
For my heart
Life was infuriating
Emotions raw
Not always pleasant
Stormy
Rocky
Those old clichés
You a Vincent
Character spread across the room
Intense streaks and swirls of vibrant pigment
I a Hemingway
Thoughts sprawled with drunken abandon
Over the page
Alive

Keeper of Her Memories

I remember her smile and her warmth
Her laughter and joy in her family
I remember hugs and a willing playmate when I
was bored
How fastidious she was about her house
Hand-sewn dresses and the curls she spent hours
putting in my hair
I remember her fussing over my wedding dress
and holding my first-born
and the love in her eyes on both occasions
I remember parties and summers in the back
yard
Trips to the beach
Barbecues and Thanksgiving turkeys
And Christmas - her favorite holiday
Her twenty-fifth anniversary, and her fiftieth,
and the sixtieth
I remember comfort when I needed it
Discipline when, too often, I deserved it
Love always, unconditional and freely given
Some of this remains

In the fog that shrouds her mind
Between the synapses that no longer fire
my mother lives and breathes but seldom peeks
out at me
The smile and warmth are still there
The laughter, more often punctuated by
frustrated tears
still remains
Sometimes she will surface through the murk
and I dare to hope, to dream
But the reality is she will not come back
only retreat further and further from all she
knew and loved
The shell is here
The rest on a sojourn I cannot make
lost in the grim wonderland of her dementia
And I am left to be the keeper of her memories

Learning You

I know the smell of your skin
And the taste that is uniquely your own on my
lips
Of woods and mist and sunshine and grass and
sea air
Sampled each time you pulled me in and let me
linger

I know the feel of your touch
And the warmth of your palms over my ears
Of your mouth against my forehead, your breath
on my neck
The weight of your arm around my shoulders

I know the measure of your eyes
And the smile that resides there for me
Of tenderness and lust and wonder and
amusement and hope
In each glance you shared

I am still learning you
but this much
I know

Mirror Mist

In the mirror's mist I watch
The-girl-I-was
She of the doe eyes and saucy breasts,
The slimness of her, the vibrance
The creamy coffee color of summer-drenched
skin

I think she does not see me
The-woman-she-will-be
I hope she does not
But she grins and I catch the roguish twitch of
one lid
And know she will not hold what-I-have-
become against me

Lightfall

Scraping.

"Jeremy?" I can't believe that sound, timid, barely a whisper, comes from my throat. Even as soft as it is, it bounces around the cavern a few times before disappearing in the direction Jeremy went when he left. I keep the picture of his retreating back firmly in mind or else I'll go crazy. Sometimes I picture the front of him coming toward me, but that's a harder one to hold on to since it hasn't happened yet.

The flashlight gave out a long time ago. I watched the light dim, becoming yellow, then orange, and then flickering before it burned away, leaving a spot on my retina that lasted a few seconds. Now I sit here in the darkness, waiting for Jeremy to come back, willing him to come back and bring the light with him.

The bone in my leg stabs if I try to move, but I remember a pool of milky water somewhere to my right and mean to drag myself over there. The thirst is constant, a product of my fear and my fever, giving me the impetus to move. The screech that burns its way over my vocal chords grates against my eardrums until I find the water and drink deep. I won't move again, except when Jeremy comes back.

I can't remember how long I've been here. Time has no meaning in the dark, but I'm sure I've slept and woken at least twice. Whether a full sleep each time, I can't guess. Without the light to guide my rhythms, I have no means of knowing.

The need to see is elemental now, one with the need to sleep, love, or laugh. I crave the light the way I crave food to eat, and have had neither in long enough for their absence to sting. Once Jeremy comes back, I'll make sure he doesn't leave me without light again for a long, long time.

Cold creeps up on me despite the fever and I shiver a little. The dampness beneath me is sticky, and I wonder if the coppery smell could mean the wet is blood. I can't imagine that so much would have come from me. The hole where the bone sticks through isn't very large at all, so it must be something else.

Scraping again. What is it?

"Jeremy?" The whisper is raspy and hard to hear. When Jeremy finally does make it back here, I won't be able to talk to him very well. But once I regain my voice, I'm going to have a few choice words to say to that boy for leaving me here so long. The injury to my leg isn't so bad that he couldn't have found some way to take me with him, even if my knee is bending the wrong way.

I can't hear the noise anymore, only the thudding of my own heartbeat in my ears, louder and louder, filling my head. The wetness I feel is crawling up my thigh and hip and I'm tempted to take off my jeans to keep it from going any higher, but I'm so cold. If I sleep for a while, maybe I'll warm up, but my thoughts won't let me sleep yet. And the strange flashes I see behind my closed eyelids mock me in my desire for even a flicker of match-glow.

No food. No blanket. No bandage for my leg. No backpack to rest my head on. Just his thin jacket and the only flashlight, a package of peanut butter and cheese crackers and this pool of nasty water. He didn't even leave me with a book of matches when he left.

I'm very angry with Jeremy, but I'd forgive him if only he'd bring the light back.

Merlin's Song

For love of his home, he dreams a castle arrayed
in mist and cloud

For love of an idea, he endures a world spiraling
into darkness

For love of the man, he weeps slow tears of
ancient sorrow

For the love of Camelot, he waits…

Soul Guardian

I remember being a girl once. Birthday parties and swimming at the rock springs, barbeques in the summer and camping trips, and sledding in the cold snows of winter. I remember a sister and two brothers, my mother and father. And love.

The news spoke of wars and world hunger, murder, robbery, rampant disease, racism, terrorism and hate. A world where mankind never changed, a planet on the verge of self-destruction that terrible autumn of the last normal year.

My parents worked for the CDC. I would hear them talking at night, when they thought we were sleeping. Their voices carried to my room through the heating ducts. I heard their bafflement over the strange symptoms and the swift onset of death, unexplained, a few days later.

They spoke of "the disease" as a riddle to solve, an enigma they played with. A curiosity not yet serious. Life went on as usual until they and the others who worked with them became desperate to find the missing puzzle pieces.

The changes began the second week, as first hundreds, then thousands fell. Schools closed. Churches filled, but God had left mankind to reap its own crop. The prayers pounded Heaven's gate and were returned, unanswered.

The run on the grocery stores started, a trickle that became a raging river. My parents did the same as everyone else, loading the van with cans that took us hours to put away. We filled the pantry and closets, as if all that food would somehow make us immune to whatever claimed our neighbors, our friends, our relatives.

It became unsafe to be out of the house after dark, and then to be out of the house at all. When the stores ran out of food, it became unsafe anywhere outside or in as people hunted for something, anything to eat. We children huddled in the bedroom, afraid to curse the parents who left us alone, waiting for the reassuring sound of our car in the night.

My mother didn't come home the fourth week, my father the week after that. My brother cared for us between calls for information about our parents, calls that after the sixth week were answered by a machine. My little sister succumbed somewhere in the third month and my youngest brother two days later. We laid them in the back yard wrapped in their bedsheets, we remaining two members of our once noisy family, in silence and with tears wetting the hard, frozen earth we couldn't dig. When my older brother died in February, I was alone.

The electricity went the first week in March, plunging the world into a darkness blacker than blindness. The flashlight batteries lasted a week or two longer, and I learned to make a fire in the fireplace to stay warm and for the light it gave. I hadn't ventured farther from the house than the back yard woodpile since the beginning, but when the food gave out that spring, I didn't have a choice.

I don't know what I expected, but the first thing I noticed was the quiet. No planes, no cars, no voices. The streets I walked were eerie in their emptiness. I was grateful for the sun's late-afternoon warmth on my face as I wandered the silent city, listening in vain through the birdsong for a human noise.

Rats scuttled from the buildings where I searched for food. Store shelves sat empty and I braved an apartment building for the cans it held, stuffing them into the pack I'd grabbed from the mudroom at home. The weight felt comforting when I settled it onto my back. Only as I left did I pause to wonder what had happened to the bodies. Even at twelve years old, I knew enough to realize that dying people would leave bodies, and that most of them would be at home. I'm not sure why the absence of those bodies didn't puzzle me more.

I must have walked five or more miles searching for anyone, alive or dead. The rain came near twilight when I had reached the park, a place I'd been forbidden to go alone in times before. That day, afraid I might be the only person alive

in the city, I sought the company of even
muggers and murderers and ventured in.

The silence was deafening in its vastness.
Animals scampered through the falling water,
but nothing larger than a squirrel. The dogs and
cats were missing, too. The rain stopped and
night closed in, the darkness around me broken
by a half moon. I'd been to the park a few times
and knew the paths, but everything seemed
strange beneath the moonlight.

That's why I didn't pay strict attention to the
glowing smudges of light dancing around the
mammoth tree trunk at first. A tree that hadn't
been there months before. A tree that shouldn't
have been there now. An ancient tree, its
branches spread out over a city block and
reaching so far toward the heavens that I
couldn't see its top. It pulsed with thousands of
tiny sparks that swirled in mesmerizing
movements.

I should have been afraid, I suppose, but I felt
nothing threatening in the dance. The urge to
get closer pushed me forward until I stood
beneath bare branches. The orbs swarmed over

me, against my skin and eyes and mouth, and still I didn't fear. Warmth enveloped me and where the glowing spheres touched, my clothing vanished until I stood naked but covered in a fairy light that melted into my body. The glow shone from beneath my skin, transforming the area under the tree into a golden grotto, and the longing of a million unborn souls filled my heart.

When morning came, I awoke in a place that no longer looked the same. The tree remained, its branches now fully leafed-out. Beyond its shelter stretched fields and mountains, as if the hand of God had swept the planet clean, replacing man's ugly concrete ramparts with nature's gifts. Beside me on the ground lay a dozen or so of the minute orbs, glistening in a stray shaft of sunlight. What strange compulsion had me digging beneath that tree I can't explain, but I planted those glowing balls of light, knowing it was right to do so.

The morning beckoned me onward, into the open fields, toward the distant mountains. I began my journey.

*****

There have been no glowing orbs by my side upon my waking for the last few days now. I am tired, as I never was before, so I know my time is near an end.

I've lived now long beyond my span of normal years. But I've come to realize that I haven't been a normal human since the night I spent beneath that great tree in Central Park.

Each dawn for the last millennia, I woke to plant yet again the souls entrusted to my care. And every morning moved on to a different place, realizing that I had crossed oceans and rivers in my sleep to spread this holy seed upon distant lands. What strange new breed will come of my labors, I will never know.

I won't see the results of my work. Whatever seeds will germinate will not do so until the last of my kind has been erased from the planet's memory.

I only hope that gentler hearts will people the earth.

Millennium

i saw your face across the room
and knew you
but we'd never met

your eyes haunt me
although i'd never looked into them before

but i have seen them in my dreams
every night for a thousand thousand years

$\mathcal{D}$ippin'

"You sure?"

We'd been building up to this for weeks now, ever since hearing Seth and the other boys talking about it. But my voice quavered.

"Dunno. You?"

Cady's voice shook worse than mine.

"Yeah."

We slithered out the window into the arms of the silver maple that rapped against the house during wind storms and dropped whirling seedpods into the garden bed. Ma thought nobody heard her cussing softly under her breath as she yanked out the baby trees that sprouted among her vegetables.

The air was still and wet with the humidity of the day past. I could feel the moisture on my skin. Sweat popped up along my hairline and trickled down the side of my face. I wiped it away with the sleeve of my nightgown.

The bark felt smooth under my feet but scraped the insides of my legs as I slid farther from the house. I clung to the branch, prepared for the way it shivered and swayed when Cady added her weight to mine.

"Marlee!!" she wailed.

"Shhhh. We're gonna get caught."

She stifled her cries, but I could see her eyes rolling white in the faint moonlight. She hated heights. She got all sweaty and pale, like that time that Pa made her climb up into the loft after her cat. About halfway up the ladder, I thought she was gonna fall, but you didn't disobey Pa, no matter what you were afraid of, 'specially with him standing there at the foot of the ladder watching.

"C'mon," I hissed, scooching into the vee formed by the branch and the tree trunk.

"I can't move."

"Then stay here 'til I get back."

It was a cruel thing to say, but sometimes you had to say stuff like that to get her going.

"Don't you leave me here," she wailed again.

"Will you *hush* and *c'mon* then?"

Inch by slow inch, she slid toward me, her knees so tight around the branch I could hear the skin peeling off her legs. Her nightgown was up near around her waist, but she was too scared to even notice. It was going to take us another twenty minutes to get down the tree at the rate she was moving.

A few scary moments and an almost broken neck later, we stood on the damp grass. Cady cried softly from the painful rough burns to the tender skin between her thighs. I wasn't sure how we were going to get her back up that tree, even if she hadn't been such a scairdy-cat about climbing it.

"Can you walk?" I asked, worried that someone would hear her crying. "Cady, can you walk?"

I saw her head jerk up and down a couple times.

"Then let's go."

We slipped across the front lawn and through the gate. The moon played peek-a-boo in the clouds, one minute lighting the way and the next plunging everything into gloomy darkness. The soft dirt road puffed up between our toes and sifted onto the hems of our nightgowns like powdered sugar on cake. Bushes rustled and creaked, and somewhere not too far off, some critter chattered and then went still. Cady's hand crept into mine and though I was three years older, I was glad of the contact.

I'd never been out alone this late at night, and never this far from the house. The familiar way seemed foreign and frightening, the darkness hiding any number of dread things. My feet moved faster of their own accord, and the shuffling sound of Cady's steps echoing mine spooked me.

By the time we neared the lake, we were almost running, our breath coming sharp and quick. Cady's palm sweated in mine. I could almost hear her heartbeat pounding in her chest the way I could hear my own pounding in my ears. Sweat smelled rank on both of us. My gown stuck to my back and legs.

Then the moon slid out of its cloudy sheath and painted a sparkling white trail across the water. I caught my breath at the sight. Fairyland, like the pictures in the red cloth books Ma had in the shelf above the rocking chair. The books were old and cracked, the fabric frayed and stringy in places, but the pictures' deep colors showed landscapes much like the one I looked at now.

I could hear the faint lapping at water's edge. If sounds could be felt, I felt that one cool and clean against my skin. I shook Cady's hand clear.

"Marlee!"

The shock in her voice stopped me with my nightgown halfway over my head. But it didn't stop me for long. With a yank, I pulled the cloth away from my sticky skin and threw it on the ground.

"I'm going in that water," I said. "What do you think we came here for?"

"But, but, you're, you don't have…"

Her voice trailed off in embarrassed silence and she looked away, out over the lake. I glanced down at myself, at the body that had changed so over the last year, at the breasts that pointed outward and the hair that had sprung up on much more of me than my head.

I could feel my face burn but I walked past her and into the water, letting it glide over my legs in a silky caress. The cold of it on my parts shocked me, and my breasts tingled and tightened when I sank up to my neck. Something deep inside me began to sing. I forgot about Cady, forgot everything as I answered the call of the water.

New York City Dreams

I have a small space there
Full of my life
Stacks of books
The computer where I write nonsense
A well-used chair
Hero, my cat, her tuxedo smooth and sleek
Her white bib shines in the morning light sliding
soft through uncurtained windows
The place smells of last night's sauce

And roses
atop the
mantle of
the only
honest-to-
god
working
wood
fireplace
in the
entire
building

I crave the peace of that room
And the anticipation of clamor on the streets
below
Like an addict, I can taste the city I can't reach
and will never have
I cry for it sometimes where no one can hear me
This place I've never been
This life I've never lived

Regrets

Thunderstorms
make me think of you
Something wild
and elemental
that brings you to mind
legs braced against the wind
the rain slanting across your face
Like the tears I cry
for what we've lost

Art Appreciation

"I have no clue what that is."

Cass tipped her head sideways, hoping her eyes would unscramble the mass of floating, colored dots in front of her into something her brain could comprehend. No luck. The framed multi-colored globs of paint remained just that.

She huffed her dark brown bangs out of her eyes. Her brother was always carrying on about "art" this and "art" that, how an appreciation of painting and sculpture could "make your soul sing" and other rubbish along those lines. He urged her to take just "one walk through an exhibit," promising that it would "totally change your life."

In order to get him off her back, Cass agreed to come out with him this weekend. No sooner had they started through this first exhibit, though, Ray had ditched her to trot along behind

one of his artistic friends and gush over truly
horrible paintings. Like this one.
Maybe if she bent over a little further…

"Careful there."

The big hands that caught her before she fell to
the floor in complete disgrace cradled her
forearms and had indigo paint imbedded along
the edges of both thumbnails.

"Thanks," Cass said. "I'm always getting
myself into situations like this."

"Falling over?"

Cass tipped her head back up to look into blue
eyes about the same color as the painted nails,
liking the way the summer-browned skin around
those eyes creased with their owner's smile.
Returning the smile, she pulled back from the
hands and straightened.

"Putting myself in ridiculous positions from
which unknown knights errant have to rescue
me because I don't believe that forces of physics
or nature apply to me, of course," Cass said, all

in one breath. "Or else saying stupid things like I just said."

"I could see where that could be a problem." His gaze took in her dark hair and the deep mocha of her eyes. "I have a thing for maidens in distress. At least I can fix the "unknown knights" part. I'm Eric."

"Cassandra. Cass." She smiled again, liking that Eric stood a few inches taller than her own five-nine height.

"Really? The name of the painting is 'Cassandra Crossing.' Isn't that weird?"

"What, this one? With all the dots?"

"You don't like it?" Eric's smile faded. Cass was reminded of the change in light when a cloud races across the sun. She suddenly remembered the paint along the edges of Eric's nails. With a sinking feeling, she knew she had just insulted his artwork.

"Oh, I'm so…it's…well…it's not that…" she stammered. Mortified, she stopped trying to talk and drew a deep breath. She felt incapable of stringing two words together intelligently, but blundered ahead, trying to apologize.

"I've really put my foot in it this time," she said. "I'm sorry. I didn't mean to insult your painting."

"My..."

Eric started laughing, a nice, gentle laughter that made his eyes crinkle again and his face come alive. If she wasn't so embarrassed, Cass would have laughed along with him. She hung her head until he was finished.

"I'm flattered you think I painted that," Eric finally said, "or at least I would be if I thought it was any good."

Cass's eyes swung up to Eric's. "It's not...you didn't..."

"That mess? Are you kidding me?" Eric laughed again and tipped his head sideways, the way Cass had done earlier. "Can't make heads or tails of it."

"But, I thought…the paint on your hands…"

"Oh, I'm a painter, all right. Own my own company, too. We do interiors and exteriors." At Cass's puzzled look, Eric said, "Houses. Interiors and exteriors. Roofing, remodeling, basement conversions, you name it."

"I was sure…" Cass began, and then stopped. She laughed a little herself. "I'm glad it's not yours."

"Are you here with anyone?" Eric asked. "I mean…"

Cass looked down the length of the gallery to where Ray was totally absorbed in a six-foot piece of sculpture that reminded Cass of an ant twisted into four dimensions.

"No one," she answered. "Want to get out of here?"

"My trusty steed is in the parking lot, if you don't mind a motorcycle."

"I have a thing for motorcycles," she said as they walked toward the door. Maybe Ray had been right. Maybe this one walk through an art exhibit would change her life forever.

There are days...

…when the sound of your voice is the only thing that can smooth the rough edges of my mind

…when only the touch of your hand calms the beast that snarls within

…when the look in your eyes will pull me from the gloom where I am lost

…when the scent of your skin replaces my city walls with freedom

…when the taste of your lips on mine sweetens the bitter sting of tears

Unexpected Roads

So many lost dreams
Fallen tears
Hopes tumbled into dust
I long for the days love was a bright spark in the
night sky
Our comet on the rise
You courted and
I could summon no resistance
Helpless before the façade of your emotion
You asked and I gave you my heart
Unconditionally
Trembling with trust
So misplaced
You did not guard it well
But handed it back to me
And left me to falter along the way

The End

No fanfare
The sky didn't fall
The sun rose and set as usual
My heart beat steady and even
I drew a breath
Breathed you out
And it was done

Turn the Page

For

Other Offerings

From

Camelot Publishing Company

A Strange Encounter at Little Hubery
By Jack C. Phillips

Seven strangers are trapped in a remote and lonely railway station on the desolate Yorkshire moors when a freak storm brings a tree down on the tracks. As railway staff battle to clear the line further north, it becomes apparent that those stranded will be there for the night, and they reluctantly settle down in the waiting room as the storm rages about the exposed moorland.

Who lurks in the dimly lit station, watching the passengers as they huddle around the fire? And what lies in wait for them outside on the storm-tossed moor? One by one, stories are told and secret revealed, and it soon becomes unnervingly evident to those seeking sanctuary at the old station that things at Little Hubery are not what they seem.

A real spine-tingler to curl up with beneath the duvet on a cold winter's night.

I Softly Went A Huntin'
and other such nonsense
By Wayne Riley

With comic discussions of 'glamping' and
tongue-in-cheek comments about why he loves
his wife, Wayne Riley's first book is a fun romp
through crazy illustrations, pun-filled short
stories and nonsense poetry that will keep you
paging from one delightful offering to the next.
Find out who-dunnit in The Case of the
Mysterious Dark-Haired Stranger or what it's
like on Another Day in Paradox. Sail with the
Tweetamol, plant a Rumplebean, and enjoy a
nostalgic trip to your childhood, where the silly
is perfectly practical.

Available from Camelot Publishing Company
on Amazon everywhere

No. 41 Burlington Road
By Jack C. Phillips

When his wife suddenly ups and leaves him without warning, Jared Colne is left severely depressed and agoraphobic and cuts himself off from his friends and family. Having no contact with the outside world and dependent upon alcohol and anti-depressants to get him through the day, Jared begins spying on his neighbours on Burlington Road, and soon finds himself living in a dark, fantasy world where nothing is as it seems. As things quickly spiral out of control, Jared realises it's not only his sanity he's in danger of losing.

Who is the pale-faced boy who watches him from beneath the lamp-post across the road? Who lurks in the shadows in the abandoned house opposite? Where does his neighbour Graham go at the dead of night? And who or what is haunting his home, filling his lonely, sleepless nights with fear and dread?

With just the right amounts of comic relief, passion, tears and creepy, tense moments, Burlington Road crosses many genres and is guaranteed to keep you hooked until the story's gripping climax.

Available now in all good bookshops
And on Amazon everywhere

Tales of the Mysterious and Macabre
By Simon Parker

Ever wonder what makes a serial killer take those first tentative steps? Or what you'd feel if a pile of rotting flesh grabbed you with putrid fingers? How psychotic would you become if you discovered hell was a real place and you were in it? Find the inky places between the shadows in these tales of psychological terror and darkest fantasy that bring the gothic tradition bang up to date.

Available now from Camelot Publishing Company on Amazon everywhere

And coming soon

Varying Degrees of Nothingness

By Jack C. Phillips

An offering
of poetry and short stories
from an exceptional author

Available in 2016 from Camelot Publishing
Company

www.ingramcontent.com/pod-product-compliance
Lightning Source LLC
Chambersburg PA
CBHW031626040426
42452CB00007B/692